Introduction

'MathsWatch' offers a structured approach to recording the outcomes of practical experiences in computation. It offers a resource of grids to support the written record of Mathematical investigation.

The handling of materials and the discussion with the teacher are essential pre-requisites to the use of such material. These sheets are not 'space fillers' that can be offered to a child without the initial support of good teaching.

A child confronted by a plain sheet of paper may have great difficulty recording particular procedures or stages in computation. The use of specific grids that offer a 'home' for each stage of a computation skill structures the process in such a manner that there is a logical connection between the practical activity and the record.

The grids are not ends in themselves, but only a supportive pattern to aid the understanding of process. The grids can provide the necessary prop during the acquisition of skill but should in the end be dispensed with as mastery is achieved.

For many children, such a detailed structure may not be required, although many of the ideas that give rise to the designing of these grids can be successfully used in mainstream teaching with all children. However, for the child who has failed to come to terms with the written record of computational activity, and for whom the plain page is an immense challenge, they provide an alternative entry and opportunity for re-motivation where previously the child has experienced defeat.

Chris McDonnell
October 1995

Two equal sets

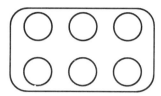

A set of 6 spots can become:

two equal sets, each with 3 spots

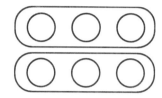

Divide each set of spots into two equal sets by drawing a line.

1. ◯ ◯
   ◯ ◯
   ◯ ◯

2. ◯ ◯
   ◯ ◯

3. ◯ ◯ ◯ ◯ ◯ ◯

4. ◯ ◯
   ◯ ◯
   ◯ ◯
   ◯ ◯

5. ◯ ◯ ◯ ◯ ◯ ◯
   ◯ ◯ ◯ ◯ ◯ ◯

Divide each set of spots into two equal sets by drawing a line.

1.

2.

3.

4.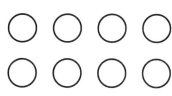

5.

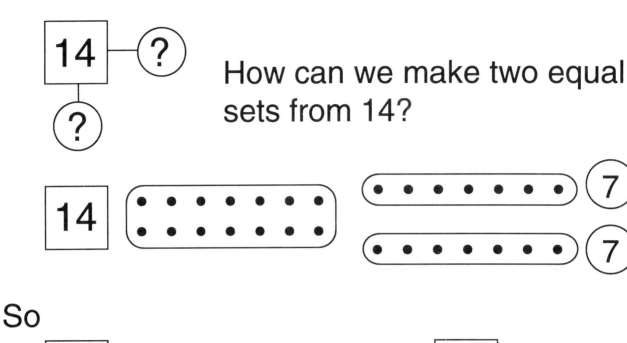

How can we make two equal sets from 14?

So

becomes ➡

14 has been divided into two equal sets, each containing 7.

Make equal sets

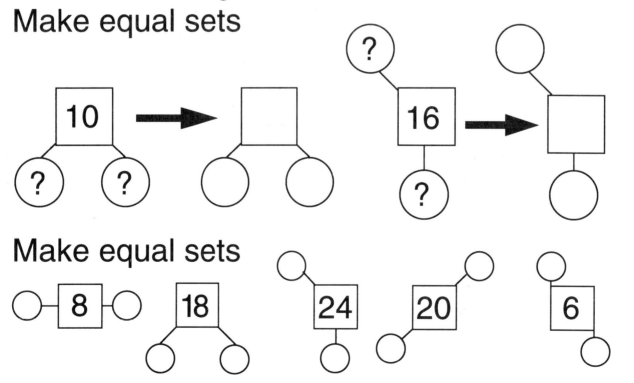

Make equal sets

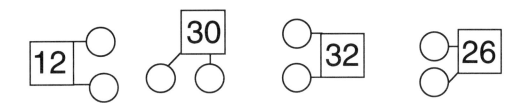

Making a set into 2 equal sets is sometimes called **'Division by 2'.** We use the sign ÷ instead of the word division.

12 ? ? → 12 6 6 → (12) ÷ (2) = (6)

16 ⬤ → ( ) ÷ ( ) = ( )

20 → ( ) ÷ ( ) = ( )

18 → ( ) ÷ ( ) = ( )

14 → ( ) ÷ ( ) = ( )

Remember the multiples of 2?

$$3 \times 2 = 6$$

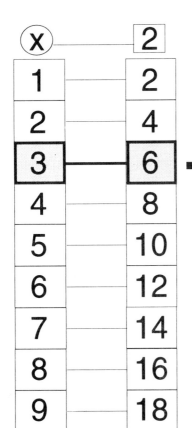

So:

6 divided by 2 is 3

$$6 \div 2 = 3$$

Division by 2

1. $10 \div 2 = \bigcirc$

2. $8 \div 2 = \bigcirc$

3. $14 \div 2 = \bigcirc$

4. $20 \div 2 = \bigcirc$

Just as:

$$2 \times 9 = 18$$

so we can make 2 equal sets:

$$9 - 18 - 9$$

and then write: $18 \div 2 = 9$

$$2 \times 7 = 14$$

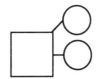 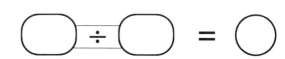

$$\bigcirc \div \bigcirc = \bigcirc$$

2 columns

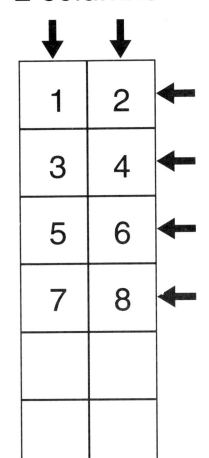

1	2
3	4
5	6
7	8

← 4 rows

Finish this table
for the multiples
of 2

$8 \div 2 =$ ◯

Division by 2

1. $16 \div 2 =$ ◯

2. ◯ $\div 2 = 10$

3. $14 \div$ ◯ $= 7$

4. $18 \div 2 =$ ◯

7

Three equal sets

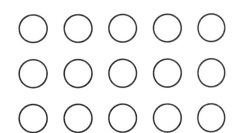 A set of 15 spots

Makes 3 sets each
of 5 spots

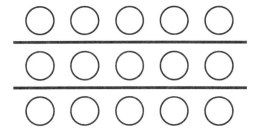

Make 3 equal sets by drawing lines:

1. ○ ○ ○
   ○ ○ ○

2. ○ ○ ○
   ○ ○ ○
   ○ ○ ○
   ○ ○ ○

Division by 3

Draw lines to show 3 equal sets

1. • • • • • • • • • •
    • • • • • • • • • •
    • • • • • • • • • •

2. • • • • •
    • • • • •
    • • • • •

3. • • •
    • • •
    • • •
    • • •
    • • •
    • • •

4. • • • • • •
    • • • • • •
    • • • • • •
    • • • • • •
    • • • • • •

5. • • •
    • • •
    • • •

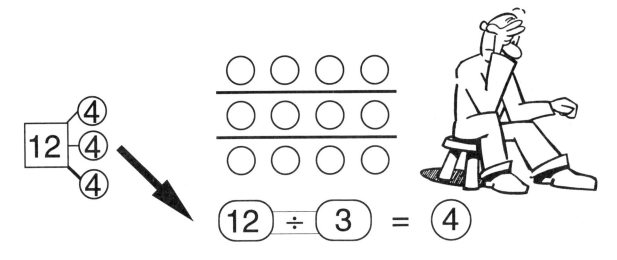

$$(12) \div (3) = (4)$$

Use a spot sheet to help you do these

○○ [21] ○ ➔ ⬭ ÷ ⬭ = ○

○ [15] ○ ○ ➔ ⬭ ÷ ⬭ = ○

○ [18] ○ ○ ➔ ⬭ ÷ ⬭ = ○

○ [30] ○ ○ ➔ ⬭ ÷ ⬭ = ○

○ [27] ○ ○ ➔ ⬭ ÷ ⬭ = ○

3 columns

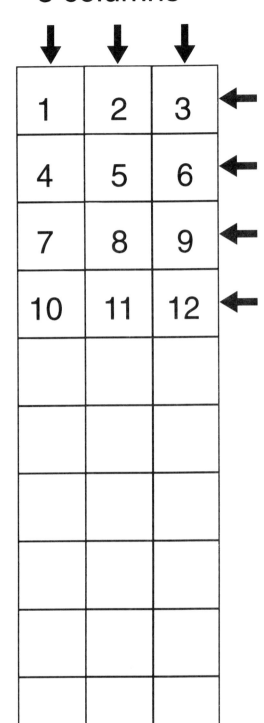

1	2	3
4	5	6
7	8	9
10	11	12

← 4 rows

Finish this table for
the multiples of 3

$12 \div 3 = 4$

Division by 3

1. $15 \div 3 = \bigcirc$
2. $21 \div 3 = \bigcirc$
3. $27 \div \bigcirc = 9$
4. $\bigcirc \div 3 = 6$
5. $30 \div \bigcirc = 10$
6. $\bigcirc \div 3 = 8$

Multiples of 3, Division by 3

x	3
1	3
2	6
3	9
4	12
5	**15**
6	18
7	21
8	24
9	27
10	30

5 sets of 3

makes 15

or:

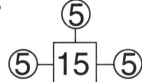

3 sets of 5 = 15

or:

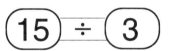

so:

Record these in the same way

1.

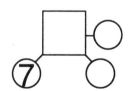

2.

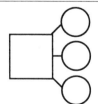

3.

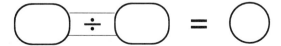

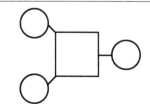

Multiples of 4, Division by 4

$\times$	4
1	4
2	8
3	**12**
4	16
5	20
6	24
7	28
8	32
9	36
10	40

(3) x (4) = (12)

or:

(4) x (3) = (12)

or: 3 — 12 — 3 / 3 — 3

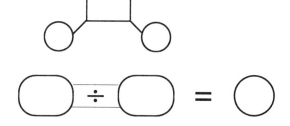

so: (12) ÷ (4) = (3)

1.

(4) x (6) = (24)

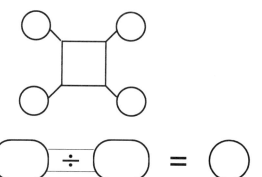

( ) ÷ ( ) = ( )

2.

(4) x (9) = (36)

( ) ÷ ( ) = ( )

(18) ÷ (3) = (6)

This can be written like this:

$$\frac{(18)}{(3)} = (6)$$

(18) ÷ (3)   means the same as $\frac{(18)}{(3)}$

(14) ÷ (2)   means the same as $\frac{(\quad)}{(\quad)}$

(24) ÷ (3)   means the same as $\frac{(\quad)}{(\quad)}$

(27) ÷ ( ) = $\frac{(27)}{(3)}$ (40) ÷ (5) = $\frac{(\quad)}{(5)}$

$\frac{(30)}{(3)}$ = (30) ÷ ( ) $\frac{(56)}{(7)}$ = ( ) ÷ (7)

$\frac{(36)}{(6)}$ = ( ) ÷ ( ) $\frac{(28)}{(4)}$ = ( ) ÷ ( )

13

$\boxed{32} \div \boxed{8} = \dfrac{\bigcirc}{\bigcirc}$ $\boxed{20} \div \boxed{4} = \dfrac{\bigcirc}{\bigcirc}$

$\dfrac{42}{0} = \bigcirc \div \boxed{7}$ $\boxed{14} \div \boxed{7} = \dfrac{\bigcirc}{7}$

$\boxed{90} \div \bigcirc = \dfrac{\bigcirc}{9}$ $\boxed{28} \div \boxed{7} = \dfrac{\bigcirc}{\bigcirc}$

Remainders..... or what is left over

$\boxed{17} \div \boxed{3}$

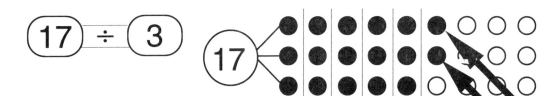

5 sets of 3 and 2 left over

$\boxed{17} \div \boxed{3}$ = 5 sets of 3 and 2 left over

$\boxed{13} \div \boxed{3}$ $\boxed{34} \div \boxed{3}$ $\boxed{26} \div \boxed{3}$

$\boxed{36} \div \boxed{3}$ $\boxed{25} \div \boxed{3}$ $\boxed{14} \div \boxed{3}$

$\boxed{32} \div \boxed{3}$ $\boxed{19} \div \boxed{3}$ $\boxed{23} \div \boxed{3}$

Look:

$3 \times 4 = 12$

so: $12 \div 3 = 4$

and: $12 \div 4 = 3$

$4 \times 7 = 28$

so: $\bigcirc \div \bigcirc = \bigcirc$

and: $\bigcirc \div \bigcirc = \bigcirc$

$5 \times 6 = 30$

so: $\bigcirc \div \bigcirc = \bigcirc$

and: $\bigcirc \div \bigcirc = \bigcirc$

Complete these, using the grid

$(8) \times (3) = (24)$

so: $(\bigcirc) \div (\bigcirc) = \bigcirc$

and: $(\bigcirc) \div (\bigcirc) = \bigcirc$

1. $(5) \times (9) = (45)$ 5. $(8) \times (4) = (32)$

2. $(6) \times (2) = (12)$ 6. $(4) \times (6) = (24)$

3. $(7) \times (5) = (35)$ 7. $(3) \times (10) = (30)$

4. $(9) \times (6) = (54)$ 8. $(2) \times (9) = (18)$

Photocopiable Grids

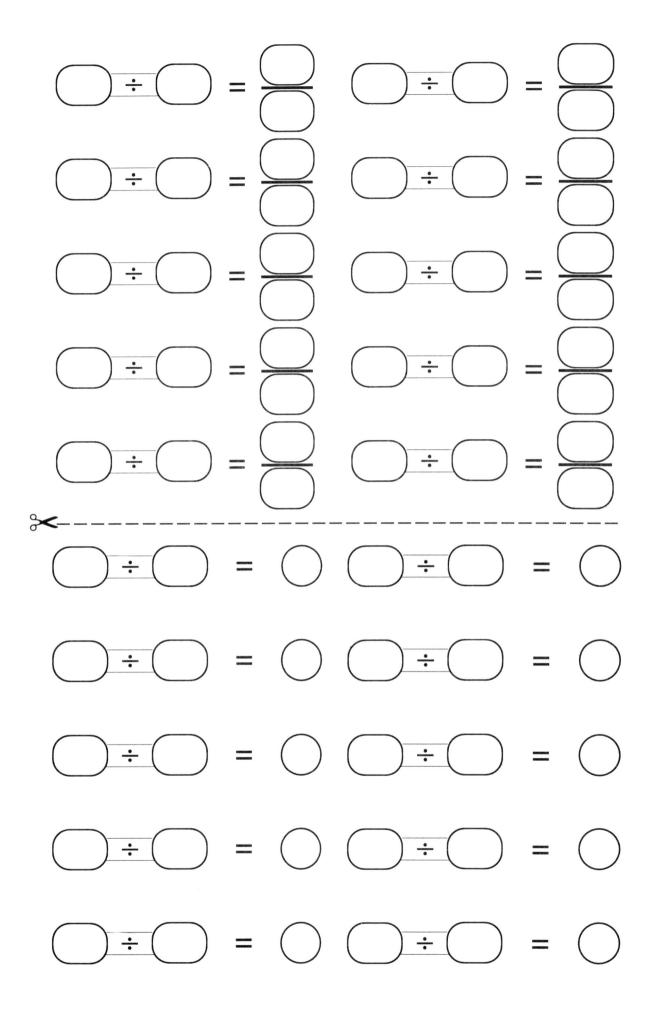

18

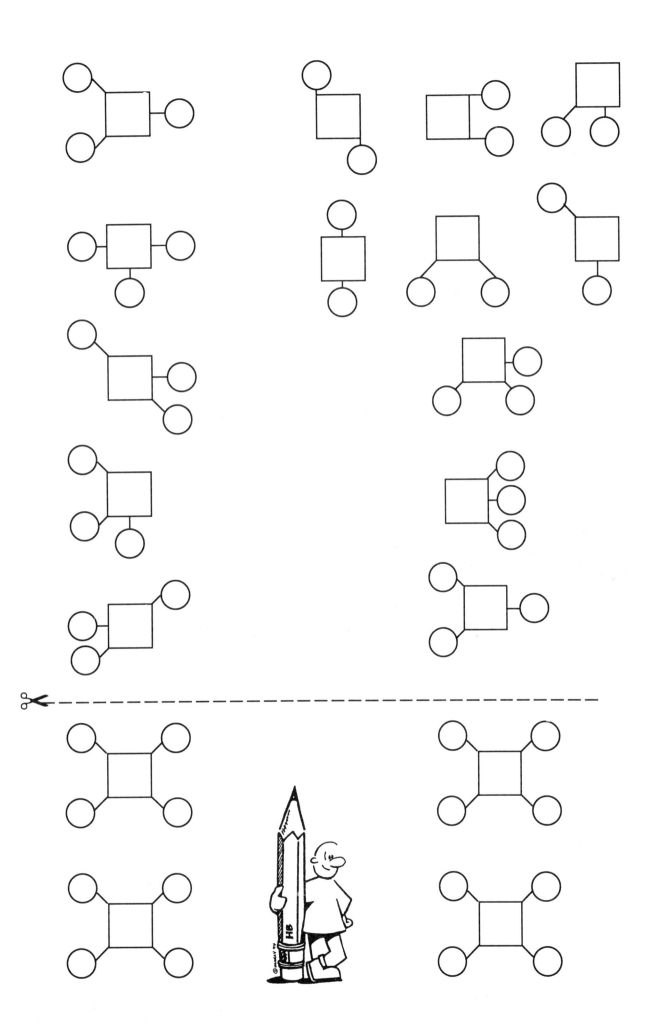

19

$\bigcirc \times \bigcirc = \bigcirc$

$\bigcirc \div \bigcirc = \bigcirc$

$\bigcirc \times \bigcirc = \bigcirc$

$\bigcirc \div \bigcirc = \bigcirc$

$\bigcirc \times \bigcirc = \bigcirc$

$\bigcirc \div \bigcirc = \bigcirc$

$\bigcirc \times \bigcirc = \bigcirc$

so: $\bigcirc \div \bigcirc = \bigcirc$

and: $\bigcirc \div \bigcirc = \bigcirc$

$\bigcirc \times \bigcirc = \bigcirc$

so: $\bigcirc \div \bigcirc = \bigcirc$

and: $\bigcirc \div \bigcirc = \bigcirc$

20

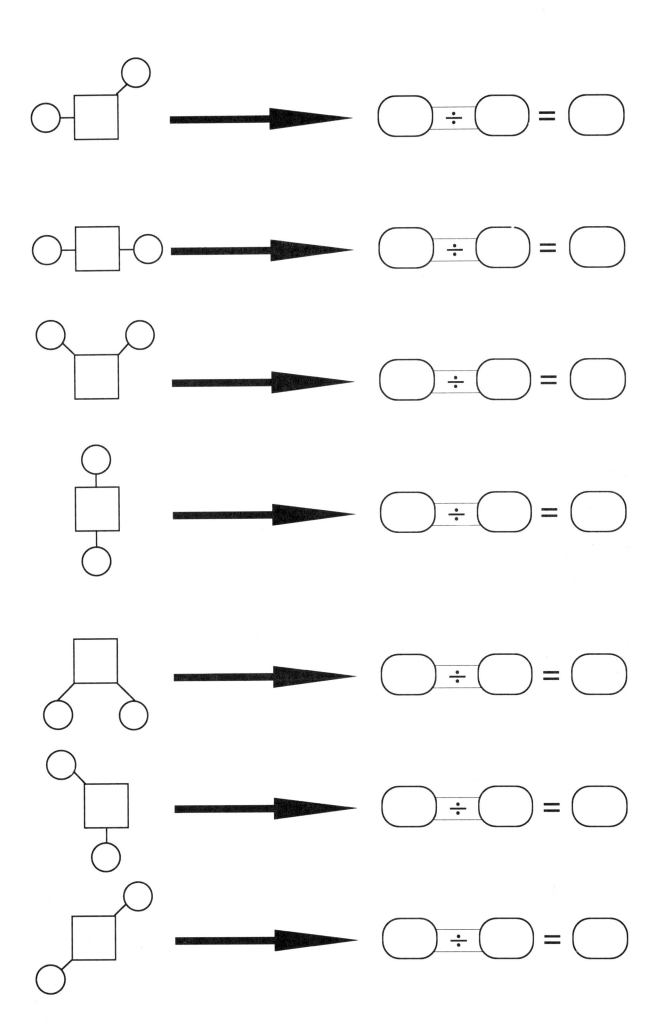

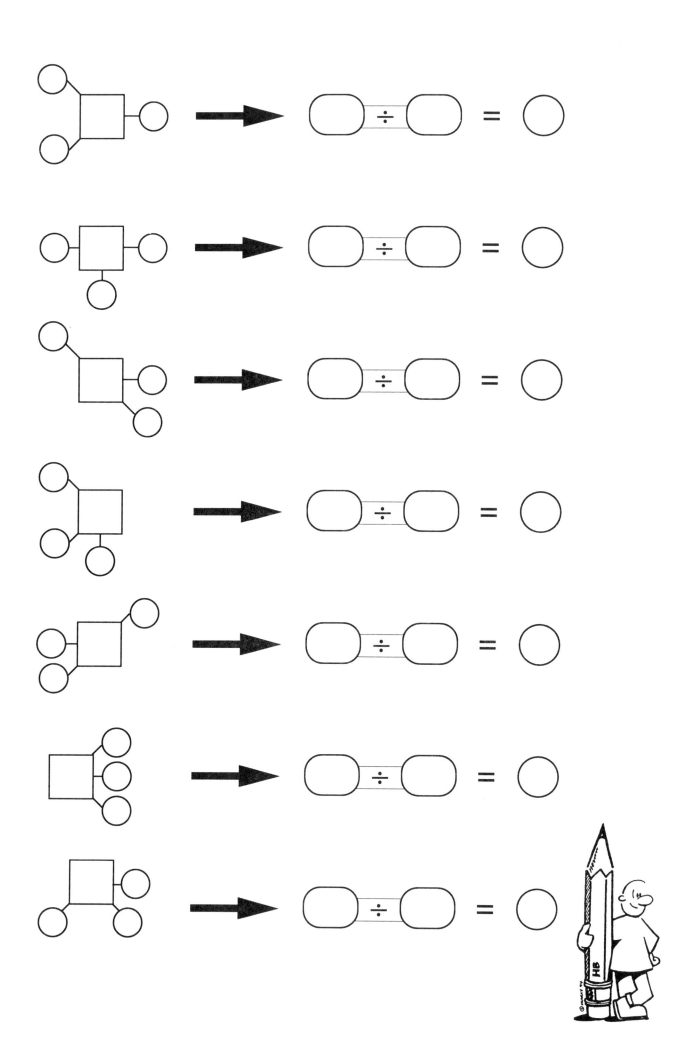

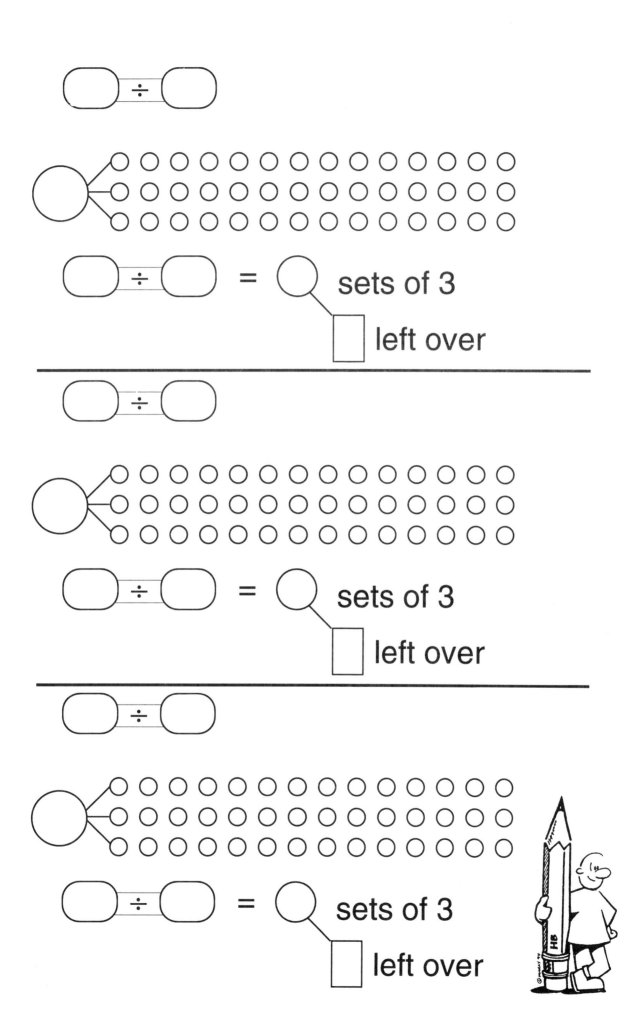

$\boxed{} \div \boxed{}$

$\boxed{} \div \boxed{} \ = \ \bigcirc$ sets of 3

$\boxed{}$ left over

$\boxed{} \div \boxed{}$

$\boxed{} \div \boxed{} \ = \ \bigcirc$ sets of 3

$\boxed{}$ left over

$\boxed{} \div \boxed{}$

$\boxed{} \div \boxed{} \ = \ \bigcirc$ sets of 3

$\boxed{}$ left over

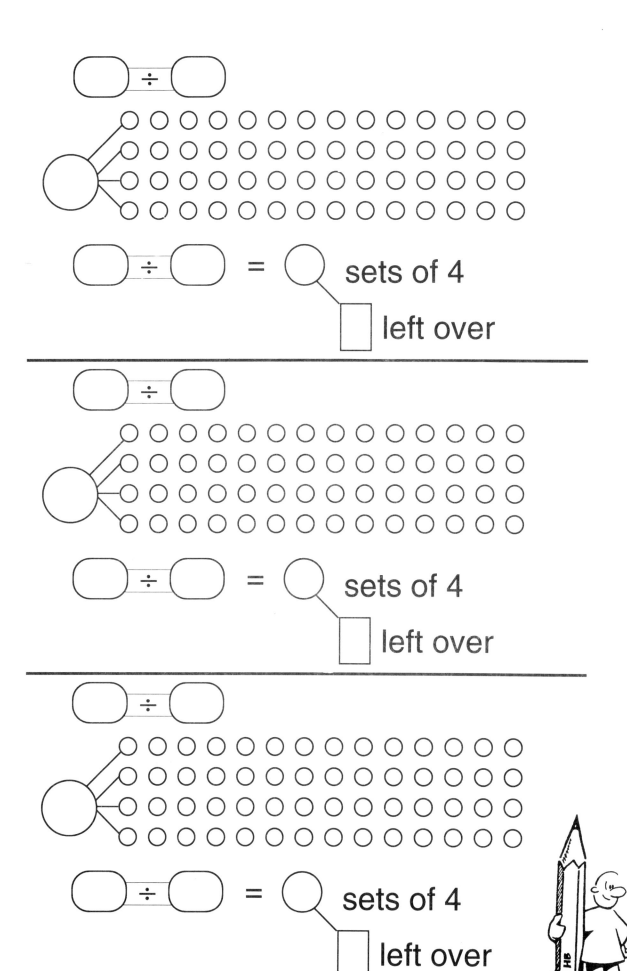

$\boxed{} \div \boxed{}$

$\boxed{} \div \boxed{} = \bigcirc$ sets of 4

$\square$ left over

$\boxed{} \div \boxed{}$

$\boxed{} \div \boxed{} = \bigcirc$ sets of 4

$\square$ left over

$\boxed{} \div \boxed{}$

$\boxed{} \div \boxed{} = \bigcirc$ sets of 4

$\square$ left over